MATHS ADVENTURES
THE MATHEMAGICIAN'S APPRENTICE

by Brian Boyd

TAG Publishing

HOW TO USE THIS BOOK AND CD

Welcome to The Mathemagician's Apprentice. In just a moment you can meet Max the Mathemagician and learn all kinds of secrets and tricks to help you get to grips with multiplication.

The aim of the book and CD-ROM is to help you learn your times tables and have great fun at the same time. The CD allows you to venture into Max's world and explore. The book is full of useful information about the times tables and gives you clues that will help you overcome the pitfalls and obstacles you may meet on the CD-ROM.

Copyright and Acknowledgements

TAG Publishing, a division of TAG Learning Ltd
9 Harmsworth St
London SE17 9TL

First published by TAG Publishing 2000
Copyright © TAG Publishing

Text and illustrations © Brian Boyd 2000
The rights of Brian Boyd to be identified as the Author have been asserted by them in accordance with the Copyright, Designs and Patents Act 1988.

ISBN 1 902 804 04 X

Reprographics by Colourwise Ltd
Printed in Hong Kong by Wing King Tong

CD-ROM Acknowledgements
Hyperstudio © Roger Wagner Publishing Inc 2000; **Windows**™ Microsoft® Corporation
Mac™, **Macintosh**™ and **Quicktime**® Apple Computer Inc

THE MATHEMAGICIAN'S TEAM
Author and illustrator: **Brian Boyd**
Design: **John Kelly**
Programming: **Tom Baird**
Production: **Landmark Ltd**
Publisher: **Kate Scarborough**
Consultant: **Justine Abbott, Numeracy Consultant, Havering LEA**

INSTALLATION
You can choose between
a minimum install or a full install.
A minimum install takes up less space on
the computer's hard disk but it
runs more slowly.
A full install takes up more hard disk
space but it will run more quickly. A full
install also allows you the option of
saving your progress as you travel
through Max's world.

FOR WINDOWS™

INSTALLATION
• Click on 'start' on the task bar
• Click on 'Run' and type
'd:\Fullsetup' (where 'd' is the letter
of your CD drive) or type 'd:\setup'
for minimum install

STARTING
• Click on 'start' on the task bar in
programs and go to
'Mathemagician'
• Click on 'Mathemagician'

FOR MAC™

INSTALLATION AND STARTING
• For a minimum install just double
click on the 'Mathemagician' icon in
the CD-ROM folder.
• For a full install, double-click on
the install icon.
• Open your hard drive and click on
the folder called 'Mathemagician'
• Double-click on 'Mathemagician'

Hello there!

My name's Max, master mathemagician and unchallenged world champion of times tables. It's great to meet you! You've just caught me thinking about my young apprentice Ozzy. He's a bright lad and shows a lot of promise, but he does have a knack for landing himself in trouble! Just last week, poor Ozzy wound up in hotter water than usual. It's my fault, I suppose. After all my training and advice, I thought he was ready for the final test of his apprenticeship...

OZZY

The journey through Straker's wood – a place where only the most expert mathematicians survive! All of my apprentices must travel through that treacherous forest alone. Straker's wood is full of dangerous creatures and enchantments ... the kind that draw their magical power from mathematics.

So why, you may ask, is multiplication so important? The truth is, multiplication is a short cut. It's a quick way of adding up lots of the same number.

For example, I'm planning to make an enormous omelette and I need to check how many dragons' eggs I have. I know I have four boxes, and that each box has six eggs in it. That's four lots of six eggs. I could work out how many eggs I have by adding up all of those sixes.

But I can do it a quicker way using the times tables.

$$4 \times 6 = 24$$

Four groups of six eggs makes twenty four eggs. Easy! And it works the other way round too. If I were to take an egg from each of the boxes, I'd have four eggs. Then I do it again....another four eggs. In fact I could do this SIX times before the boxes were empty. So that's six lots of four eggs, or

$$4 + 4 + 4 + 4 + 4 + 4$$

But 6 x 4 = 24 is so much easier!

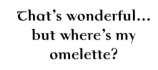

That's wonderful... but where's my omelette?

Ozzy was excited when I told him he could turn long, boring addition into quick multiplication short cuts (he'll do anything to make his work easier). And it wasn't long before he had to do just that...

As he followed the forest path, Ozzy came to a towering wooden door. This was the famous Portal of Pairs. Very powerful magic had locked this door. The only way to break the spell was to tap on two panels of the door to reveal matching sums. Uncovering the pairs would unlock the portal. Ozzy started with a heavy sigh. This could take forever. But as the panels opened and shut he began to notice something .... one panel had the sum 5 + 5 + 5. Another had 3 x 5. That's when the gold coin dropped! Ozzy realised that 3 x 5 was the multiplication short cut for 5 + 5 + 5!

Perhaps this isn't going to be so hard....

Once through the Portal of Pairs, Ozzy began to wander through the trees, deeper and deeper into Straker's wood. With his mind on other things, it wasn't long before he became hopelessly lost. Nothing seemed familiar. If it wasn't for the fact that he knew his times tables quite well, I'd have been worried about him.

Actually, the times tables aren't as difficult to learn as some people think. It seems daunting at first because there are just so many of them. Take a look at this grid here ... it has all of the times tables from 1 x 1 up to 10 x 10 in one handy picture (I've kept in the one times tables even though everybody in the world knows those ... even goblins).

Hey, thanks for the compliment... I think...

	1	2	3	4	5	6	7	8	9	10
1	1	2	3	4	5	6	7	8	9	10
2	2	4	6	8	10	12	14	16	18	20
3	3	6	9	12	15	18	21	24	27	30
4	4	8	12	16	20	24	28	32	36	40
5	5	10	15	20	25	30	35	40	45	50
6	6	12	18	24	30	36	42	48	54	60
7	7	14	21	28	35	42	49	56	63	70
8	8	16	24	32	40	48	56	64	72	80
9	9	18	27	36	45	54	63	72	81	90
10	10	20	30	40	50	60	70	80	90	100

Using this grid couldn't be more simple. Say you want to work out six times eight (6 x 8). Look along the top edge to find eight. Point to it. Now look down the left side to find six. Point to that too with your other hand. Got them? OK ... now you need to slide your fingers down from the eight and across from the six till they meet. And that's your answer – 48! It really is that easy. Try another ... let's say 9 x 5. Find the nine on the top of the grid and point to it. Now the five on the left hand side. Slide them down and across until they meet. I bet you got 45! You'll find the grid a great help while you're still learning the times tables. And you'll need to use it less and less as those tricky tables begin to stick in your head.

I usually start my apprentices off on the very easiest times tables and they don't come much easier than the two times tables. Look at the multiplication grid on page 9. If you look along the two times tables you'll see that multiplying a number by two just means doubling it.

It works for any number you want to multiply by two. Look at your hands … five fingers on each hand. That's two lots of five (2 x 5) which makes a total of ten… and ten is just five doubled. One good way of practising the two times tables is to count up to twenty in steps of two. How quickly can you do it? The two times tables can be very useful since so many things come in sets of two … as Ozzy found out in his next encounter in Straker's wood.

2
4
6
8
10
12
14
16
18

There's something odd going on here...

TOP TIP
You'll notice that all of the answers in the twos are even numbers. So if you're multiplying by two and you get an odd number for an answer, you've gone wrong somewhere.

2 x 2 = 5?

After all that wandering, the trees gradually thinned out and Ozzy found himself at a small but neat garden. Inside the fence were various plots, each containing the same curious-looking plants. "Now what have we got here?" Ozzy asked himself, reaching out to pick one. "Twinberries! And don't touch, thank-you-very-much!" came a cross reply from nowhere. Ozzy looked up with a start to see a stern-looking scarecrow frowning down at him. "Twinberries? You mean these are twinberry trees?" Ozzy asked.

THAT'S RIGHT, TWO TWINBERRIES FROM EACH TREE!

"So let's see..." began Ozzy looking at the first bed, "three trees in here and each will grow two fruits when the season begins ... that's six fruits all together!" "Smart work!" beamed the scarecrow "maybe you could help me label all of these plots, so that I'll know exactly how many fruits each bed will give me?" Ozzy, happy to take a break, began to count and label the trees. It didn't take long and the grateful scarecrow directed him on his way.

Thanking the scarecrow, Ozzy was pleased to be making progress again. He was also glad that the journey had been so easy up until now. But things were about to become trickier as he would soon need to use his three and four times tables ... both at the same time!

The threes and fours are a bit more difficult, but when you've mastered these, you know you're really on your way. Have a look at them on the multiplication grid. Try memorising them, closing the book and seeing how many you can remember. It gets easier with practice. Now see how quickly you can count up to thirty in steps of three. (Sometimes this is easier if you get some counters or buttons and put them into groups of three.) You'll find it's faster using multiplication. While looking at the three and four times tables, you may have noticed that 3 x 4

DOUBLE TROUBLE
You can multiply by four by multiplying by two twice. So for 4 x 5 do 2 x 5 (the answer is 10 of course) then 2 x 10 ... giving you 20! Some people find this useful and others find it makes things more complicated ... you decide.

Buttons and counters... what about juicy beetles in groups of three?

and 4 x 3 have the same answer ... 12.
The brilliant thing is that this works for
all of the times tables. You can swap
them around and still get the same
answer. So, if you can remember that 9 x 7 is
63, you'll know what 7 x 9 is. Two sums for the price
of one! It's a pity Ozzy didn't remember that rule. He might
have saved himself some time puzzling over his next problem...

The woods had become much more dense and thorny and up ahead the pathway was completely blocked by two trees, their branches intertwined. It seemed almost impossible to get through. Suddenly Ozzy saw that the tree on the left had flowers growing in clusters of three while the other had its flowers in groups of four.

He felt sure there was a way through and he suspected it was something to do with those flowers...

By the time Ozzy had discovered the secret of the tree barrier, it was mid-afternoon. The sun was high in the sky and here and there it shone down through the canopy of leaves above. So imagine Ozzy's surprise when he noticed tendrils of yellow fog rising from the leaves at his feet. Thicker and thicker it grew, swirling and dancing its way up. In no time it was all about him, blocking his vision. It didn't take long for Ozzy to put two and two together. Fog and sunny days just didn't go together. There was sorcery involved here and the only wizard capable of such a powerful spell (apart from his fantastic teacher, Max, of course) was Grimlock – the nastiest, meanest, most unpleasant magician ever.

Luckily, Ozzy knew a few things about this kind of spell that could be useful. Firstly, he knew that all weather spells are woven using the five and six times tables together ... and that they can be undone using those tables too. Secondly, he knew that Grimlock himself must be hiding somewhere within the fog. If he could find Grimlock, he could break his concentration and cause the spell to fail.

Mastering the five times tables isn't very hard at all. Count up to fifty in steps of five a few times. Do you notice how all of the answers in the five times tables end in a five or a zero? Remembering that can be very useful, as you know the answer you're looking for can't end in any other number.

The six times tables are a bit more tricky, but let's take a look at them. Well, six times two is twelve ... that's easy to remember because if you roll two sixes with dice you score twelve points. I can always remember that ten sixes are sixty and one six is six! That only leaves seven sums to learn in the six times tables.

AND ANOTHER...
Remember, if you know your five times tables, then 5 x 6 is 30. So, 6 x 5 is 30 too.

Oh yes! Two for the price of one again!

Slowly but surely as Ozzy worked, the fog began to thin and there crouched Grimlock, his face as black as thunder. He let out a cry of rage, waved his fist and stomped into the undergrowth. "You haven't seen the last of me!" he bellowed as he vanished from sight. Ozzy grinned and shook his head. Couldn't villains ever think of anything original to say?

As he pressed on, Ozzy began to recognise his surroundings. This was a part of the forest he knew well and since he was making good time he decided to visit a few of his old friends.

His first stop was the sweet shop owned by Jinny Greenteeth the retired witch. Although she still looked frightening, she was really very friendly. Ozzy found Jinny in a bit of a flap. She had made up several bags of sour-newt-eyes and was having trouble working out the prices of each. "I know that one packet of sour-newt-eyes costs seven gold coins" she said, exasperated, "but how can I work out the cost of a bag with three packets of sour-newt-eyes?" "Oh, that shouldn't be too difficult," smiled Ozzy "...with a little bit of multiplication magic!" He took the first bag from Jinny and made a quick count of its contents. "Now let's see ... three packets of sweets that cost seven gold coins each ... that's three lots of seven. EASY! 3 x 7 is 21!". A short time later the final bag was counted and Ozzy was on his way again. He whistled his way along in the warm sunshine as he headed to the cave of Knucklebone the troll.

A delicious smell wafted from the cave entrance and Ozzy called out a friendly hello. Knucklebone was delighted to see him, especially since he too had a problem. "I'm trying to make some of my famous stew," he explained, "but I just can't get the number of spiders' legs right." Knucklebone had already labelled each pot with the number of legs it needed, but he kept losing count while he was adding them. "I think your problem is that you're counting each leg separately," said Ozzy thoughtfully. "If each spider has eight legs, why don't you count them in groups of eight?"

"I would," mumbled the troll, "but I never learned my eight times tables."

"Don't worry, this won't take long," sighed Ozzy, as he gingerly began to count the hairy spiders into the pots.

Actually, it's no wonder that Jinny and Knucklebone had such problems with their seven and eight times tables. A lot of people get stuck with those. But what a lot of people don't realise is that there's a secret way to remember lots of the harder tables. Follow me and I'll show you what to do!

Can I come too?

MAX'S MARVELLOUS MULTIPLICATION MAGIC

This trick is fantastic and the strange thing is that not many people know it. It might seem a bit complicated at first, but once you've got the hang of it you'll see it's as easy as falling in a duck pond.

You start by holding your hands up in front of you with your thumbs pointing up and your fingers outstretched. Now you have to imagine that each of your fingers has a number on it. Your thumbs are number six, your index fingers are number seven, your middle fingers are eight and so on. You might find it helpful to stick little labels to your fingers, like this...

Well, how is this going to help me?

Now touch together two fingers which have numbers you want to multiply. As an example let's try 8 x 7 ... touch them together like this on the left.

You have to imagine your fingers split into two groups ... the top and the bottom. For now, concentrate on the top group ... that's all the fingers above the two which are touching including those that are touching. Count how many fingers are in the top group (five in this case). That's going to be

Now the clever bit comes in two parts.

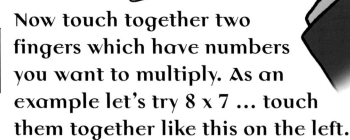

the 'tens' part of your answer so memorise it or write it down. Now to find the 'units' part. Look at the bottom group of fingers (that's everything underneath the touching fingers but not including the touching fingers). To get the units you just multiply the number of fingers on the left of the bottom group with the number of fingers on the right of the bottom group. So that's three times two, 3 x 2 = 6. Finally just pop the tens and units together ...

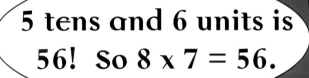

5 tens and 6 units is 56! So 8 x 7 = 56.

The best way to learn this trick is to try it lots of times using different numbers. You could use the multiplication grid on page 9 to check your answers.

Oh! There's one more thing ... like a lot of my tricks, this one goes a bit wonky sometimes. If you try doing 6 x 6 or 7 x 6 you'll notice something bizarre happens. Can you see what's going on? The trick is still working, but not in the normal way. Can you work out why it's happening and how to fix it?

AND TO SUM UP...
Here's a speedy way of describing what to do again. Just remember that you count up the fingers in the top group to get the tens and you multiply the left and right sides of the bottom group to get the units.

In the meantime, Ozzy was pressing on with his journey. He didn't fancy the idea of being in the forest when darkness fell and there was still some distance to cover. He began to smell the most awful stink and from somewhere up ahead came a gloopy bubbling sound. He pushed through some low branches and there ahead of him was a murky swamp. A wooden sign read "Ye Swamp of Misery" but Ozzy needed no introduction. Everyone for miles had heard of this disgusting quagmire.

YE SWAMP OF MISERY

The story went that anyone who fell into the swamp would never be able to feel happy again. Ozzy heaved a sigh. It would take hours to walk around the edge of the swamp. Just then, a small round head blooped to the surface and blinked at him. Then another ... and another. Of course! The only creatures who could live in the swamp were the nine-times-turtles. And Ozzy seemed to remember hearing that they would help anyone who knew their favourite tables ... the nine times tables!

Which was lucky for Ozzy since there are lots of tips for the nine times tables... let's take a look.

First of all take a look at the multiplication grid. Do you notice the pattern in the nine times tables? The units go down by one each time, while the tens go up one at a time – 09 18 27 36 45 … and so on! Another neat little trick here is to add a zero to the number you're multiplying by nine and then take that same number away from your answer. For example … 8 x 9. Add a 0 to the 8 to get 80. Now take 8 away from 80 to get 72 … 8 x 9 = 72. And this works for all the numbers in the nine times tables.

But the best trick is one that uses your fingers. Hold them up in front of you and count along from the left until you reach the number you want to multiply by nine. As an example let's try 4 x 9… count along your fingers until you reach four, and bend it down like this. Now all you do is count the number of fingers to the left of it to get the tens part of the answer and all of the fingers on the other side to get the units. In this case we have 3 and 6 which popped together makes 36! Practise it a few times, multiplying different numbers by nine.

Now that's amazing! Your fingers are pretty useful…

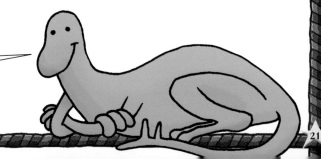

21

Soon Ozzy was on his way once more. Feeling sure he knew his way, he decided to leave the path and take a short cut through the trees. Big mistake! With a menacing hiss an enormous snake rose up in front of him. Ozzy was terrified. He didn't dare move. Then he heard an evil chuckle from the gloomy undergrowth. Grimlock! So this giant serpent was just an illusion conjured up by Grimlock to stop him succeeding! Ozzy knew what he had to do ... by finding Grimlock in the undergrowth he could ruin his concentration and stop the spell. But where to begin? The snake hissed again and its tongue flickered. In its eyes Ozzy could see numbers twinkling ... a 10 and an 8. It seemed that Grimlock was using the power of the ten times tables now.

This is the easiest multiplication short cut of them all. You only need to look at the ten times tables on the multiplication grid and you'll probably spot it straight away.

If you want to multiply a number by ten you just add a zero to the end of it. So 6 times 10 is 60, 3 times 10 is 30, 10 times 10 is 100 and so on...

And guess what? It doesn't stop at the ten times tables. This brilliant rule works for any whole number in the universe. So if you want to times 3,665,492 by 10 you just add a zero to the end of it!

You can even use this rule to help with big sums like 80 x 50! All you do is forget about the zeros for now. Which leaves 8 x 5 ... (the answer to that is 40 in case you didn't know). Now just put the two zeros back on. You get 40 and a 0 and another 0 which makes 4,000!

The ten times tables

The snake wavered and faded into thin air as Grimlock's magic failed for the second time that day. Ozzy leapt off through the trees with Grimlock's furious curses ringing in his ears.

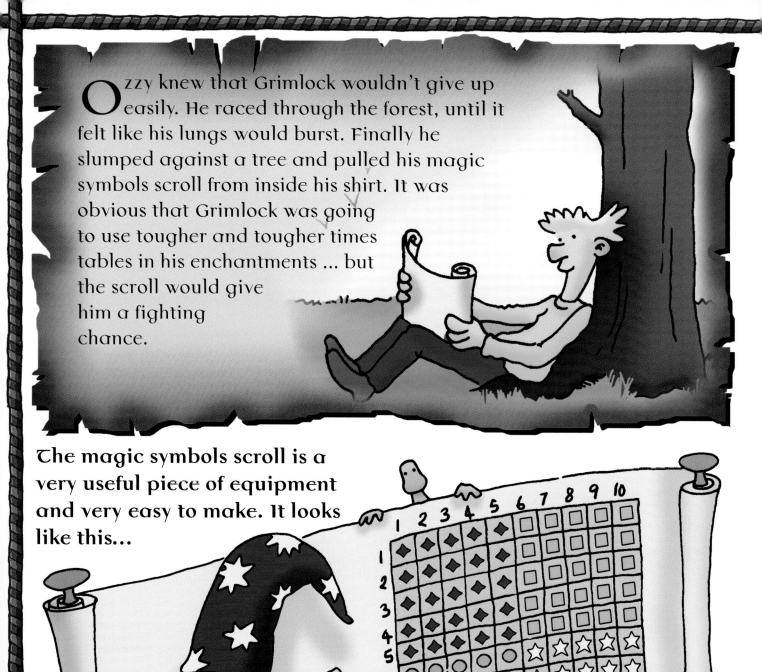

Ozzy knew that Grimlock wouldn't give up easily. He raced through the forest, until it felt like his lungs would burst. Finally he slumped against a tree and pulled his magic symbols scroll from inside his shirt. It was obvious that Grimlock was going to use tougher and tougher times tables in his enchantments ... but the scroll would give him a fighting chance.

The magic symbols scroll is a very useful piece of equipment and very easy to make. It looks like this...

It works a bit like the multiplication grid. You need two sheets of paper with straight edges and a copy of the magic symbols scroll. You also need to be able to count up in steps of five.

Let's try an example ... how about 8 x 6. Start by finding the eight on the top row of numbers. Lay a sheet of paper on the scroll so that the eight can be seen but the numbers higher are hidden. Then find the six on the side of the scroll. Same thing here ... as you can see in the picture below.

All you do now is count up all the groups of five objects you can see, and add on any extra.

Surely it can't be that easy?

In this case we have five groups of red diamonds, three groups of blue squares and one group of green circles. This makes nine groups of five, which equals forty-five. Then there are three spare stars which you just add on to the total to make forty-eight. So 6 x 8 = 48!

Practise using the magic symbol scroll as much as you want and use the multiplication grid to check your answers.

PRINT YOUR OWN
You can print your own magic symbols scroll to colour and use. Just go to the bookcase in my cottage.

It wasn't long before Grimlock caught up with Ozzy and trapped him with yet another fiendish spell. Vines from the forest floor began to move with a life of their own and wrapped themselves around his ankles. Grimlock, it seemed, would stop at nothing to trap the poor apprentice. Luckily Ozzy knew this spell well ... he had tried to use it himself once (with disastrous results!). The spell drew its power from square numbers and a good knowledge of the square numbers could help to break it.

I suppose I should explain a little bit about the square numbers.

Basically, these are the numbers you get when you multiply a whole number by itself. For example, sixteen is a square number because four times four is sixteen. And twenty five is a square number because it is five times five. It's simple really and when you multiply a number by itself you say it has been 'squared'. So six squared is the same as saying six times six.

Turn to the multiplication grid and look at all of the square numbers up to one hundred (actually one hundred is a square number itself ... ten times ten). Cover each square number with a button or a counter. What do you notice about the pattern they make on the multiplication square?

Look at how I've arranged these gold coins. Do you see why we call them square numbers?

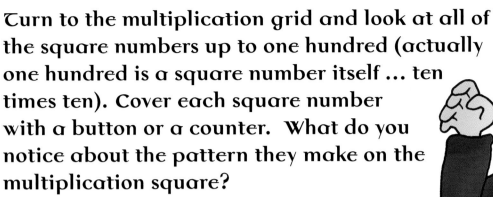

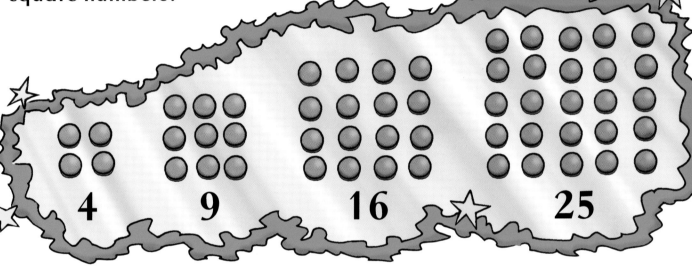

4   **9**   **16**   **25**

Ozzy, remembering his square numbers, called out the first one. Grimlock's power began to waver. With a loud snap, one of the vines broke loose. He called out the next highest square number and another vine twanged loose. Grimlock howled with fury as he realised that his magic was failing him for the third time that day. Ozzy gritted his teeth and continued to unravel the enchantment.

With the vines untangled and Grimlock thwarted Ozzy was soon racing through the trees once again. He crashed through bushes, leaped ditches and stumbled over tree roots. Before he knew it he had lost his bearings ... which way was north? Which was south?

"Need some help, my friend?" came a nearby voice. Ozzy spun around to see a fox sitting on a tree stump, smiling at him and whisking his tail to and fro. "Oh it's you, Gideon!" he said "And you want to help me? At what price 1 wonder?"

"I just need a small favour," smiled the quick brown fox. "If you help me build a tower to reach those juicy grapes up there, I'll let you go through my burrow. It's a shortcut to the forest's edge, you know."

"That sounds fair, Gideon," said Ozzy hesitantly. "All right, where do 1 begin?" The fox nodded to a pile of boxes, "first get that box with an area of twenty eight."
"An area? What's an area?" asked Ozzy blankly.
Gideon sighed and began to explain.

Finding areas is one of the many uses for times tables. If you want to work out the area of a square or rectangle you just have to multiply the two sides together. You can see for yourself how this works. Get a piece of squared paper and draw a rectangle that is nine squares long and six squares wide. Now count up how many little squares make up your rectangle all together. Did you get fifty four? Now use the multiplication grid to work out 9 x 6 .... ta daaaa! Now try it again. This time draw a square that is eight boxes long and eight boxes wide. So 8 x 8 is what? Yes, 64, and this should remind you of square numbers.

It all looks too much like hard work to me.

Ozzy caught on quite quickly too and soon that lazy old fox had him lifting and stacking the boxes into a tower.

Hee hee!

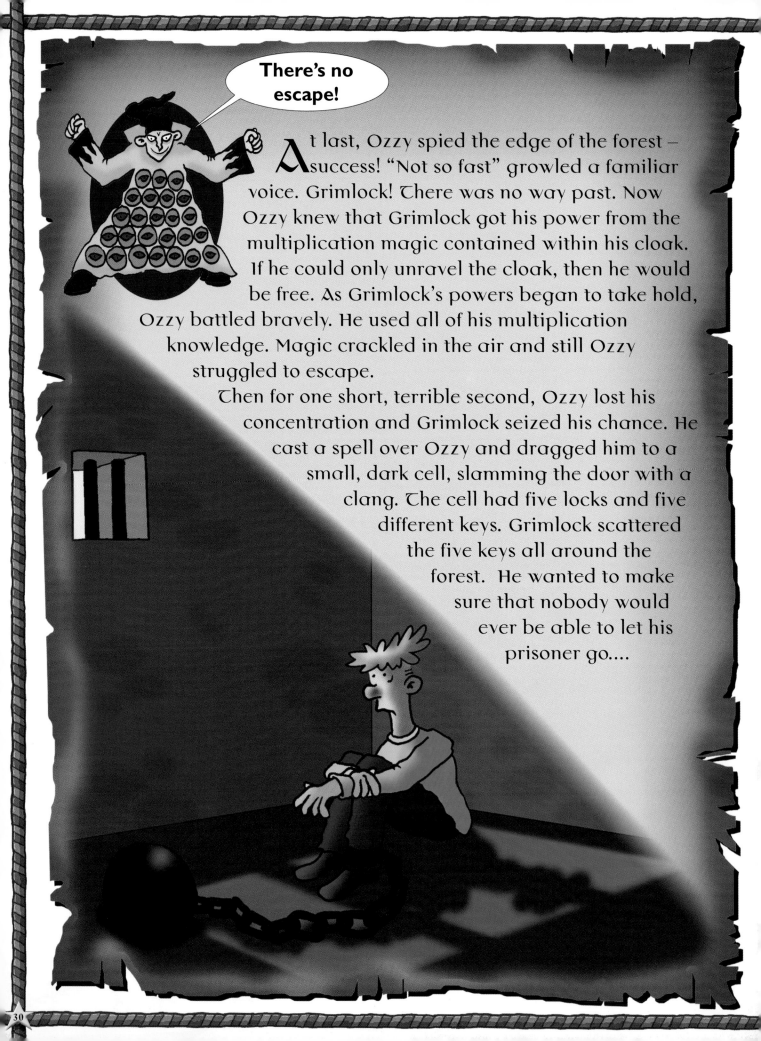

There's no escape!

At last, Ozzy spied the edge of the forest — success! "Not so fast" growled a familiar voice. Grimlock! There was no way past. Now Ozzy knew that Grimlock got his power from the multiplication magic contained within his cloak. If he could only unravel the cloak, then he would be free. As Grimlock's powers began to take hold, Ozzy battled bravely. He used all of his multiplication knowledge. Magic crackled in the air and still Ozzy struggled to escape.

Then for one short, terrible second, Ozzy lost his concentration and Grimlock seized his chance. He cast a spell over Ozzy and dragged him to a small, dark cell, slamming the door with a clang. The cell had five locks and five different keys. Grimlock scattered the five keys all around the forest. He wanted to make sure that nobody would ever be able to let his prisoner go....

And that's where the story ends. Even now, Ozzy is sitting in that cold, damp cell. But it doesn't have to end like this. You could go to the forest, find the keys and release Ozzy! But I should warn you, the forest is a dangerous place and Grimlock is still lurking there. You will need to use all the skills I have taught you to survive the traps and puzzles you'll encounter.

The disc I have provided will transport you to my cottage at the edge of the forest. I will give you a map to guide you in your search for Ozzy. You'll need to find the five keys that will release him. I'll always be there to help you if you need me.

I hope you've had fun learning the times tables and I hope my tips and secrets will help you to free Ozzy. You know that you can always come back to the book for help. And remember, it's not as difficult as it looks...............

GOOD LUCK!

GLOSSARY AND INDEX

TAG Publishing
9 Harmsworth St
London SE17 3TL
Tel: 020 7582 8341

http://www.tagpublishing.co.uk/